# LET'S LEARN ABOUT COMPUTER SCIENCE

# DATA AND DATABASES

## Jeff Mapua

**Enslow Publishing**
101 W. 23rd Street
Suite 240
New York, NY 10011
USA

enslow.com

# WORDS TO KNOW

**collection** A group of similar things.

**data** Information that is used in a computer.

**database** A collection of data.

**data processing** Putting data into a computer so that it can be used to get a result.

**delete** To take away or get rid of.

**information** Facts or things that we know.

**organize** To put in order.

**query** A request for data or information from a database.

**store** To save or keep.

# CONTENTS

Computers hold lots of information called data.

# Data

Computers work with **data**. Data is the **information** that a computer uses. This can be many things. E-mail, files, games, pictures, and videos are all kinds of data.

## FAST FACT

Data used to be stored on huge computers. Some were as big as refrigerators!

**A computer from the 1950s. Computers have gotten much smaller since then!**

# Storage

The computer changes data into numbers. The computer can read the numbers. The numbers are kept on the computer. The computer finds the data when it needs it.

## FAST FACT

We can store 60 million times more data today than we could fifty years ago.

**People enter data into computers. Computers can do many different things with the data.**

# Data Processing

**Data processing** is changing the data so the computer can use it. A person puts the data into the computer. The computer changes the data. Now it's ready for the computer to use.

**Files on a computer are like regular files. They are arranged so the computer can find them easily.**

# Databases

A **database** is a **collection** of data. Computers have a special way to **organize** databases. This makes it easy for computers to search for what they need. They can find the data quickly.

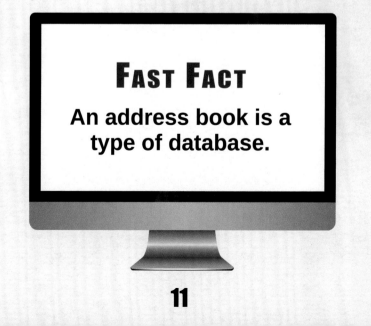

## FAST FACT

An address book is a type of database.

**Office workers put data into a database.**

# Database Processing

People can work with the data in a database. They can do a search. They can put in new data. They can **delete** data. They can also change the data.

When you go to the bank,
a computer has your
information in a database.

# Types of Databases

Some databases store words or names. Others are for numbers. A database can keep track of money. Databases are used for online shopping. People use databases at home, too.

## Fast Fact

Putting data into a computer is called data entry.

Library users can find books using a database.

# Uses for Databases

Databases can be used to store a lot of information. They can keep track of what the weather is like each day. Schools can use databases for student grades.

## FAST FACT

**The library uses a database to help you find books.**

# Databases can be tables like this one. It is set up in rows and columns.

| No. | Marketing Budget | Categories | Unit | Dec-15 | Jan-16 | Feb-16 | Mar-16 | Apr-16 | May-16 | Jun-16 | Jul-16 |
|---|---|---|---|---|---|---|---|---|---|---|---|
| 10460 | Benefits | 1-Personnal | 0 | 12,034 | 13,565 | 10,674 | 13,095 | 16,392 | 12,357 | 20,775 | 24,766 |
| 35246 | Payroll taxes | 1-Personnal | 0 | 345 | 347 | 154 | 1,953 | 374 | 534 | - | - |
| 76745 | Salaries | 1-Personnal | 1 | 521 | 434 | 178 | 519 | 1,850 | 543 | 764 | 133 |
| 76023 | Commissions and bonuses | 1-Personnal | 0 | 0 | 2,300 | 189 | 90 | 23 | 456 | 246 | 346 |
| 23674 | Personnel Total | 1-Personnal | 1 | 12,900 | 16,646 | 11,195 | 15,657 | 18,639 | 13,890 | 25,326 | 25,599 |
| 14678 | Web Research | 2-Marketing | 2 | 6,000 | 2,300 | 5,000 | 1,500 | 1,200 | 1,266 | 1,500 | 4,600 |
| 10567 | Independent Reaearch | 2-Marketing | 1 | 2,000 | 5,420 | 3,000 | 2,100 | 900 | 580 | 4,252 | 3,674 |
| 96643 | Firm Research Fees | 2-Marketing | 0 | 8,200 | 4,900 | 2,000 | 8,000 | - | 4,500 | 6,800 | 7,550 |
| 17695 | Market Research Total | 2-Marketing | 3 | 16,200 | 12,620 | 10,000 | 14,600 | 10,100 | 5,312 | 10,252 | 15,074 |
| 94015 | Promotions | 3-Commu | 2 | 1,239 | 190 | 1,245 | 432 | 134 | 357 | 2,466 | - |
| 75321 | Branding | 3-Commu | 1 | 522 | 431 | 573 | 323 | 612 | 453 | 355 | - |
| 95235 | Web Advertising | 3-Commu | 1 | 10,432 | - | 10,430 | 14,093 | 12,890 | 13,555 | 24,890 | 45,780 |
| 32564 | Direct Marketing | 3-Commu | 0 | - | 532 | 156 | 1,090 | 234 | 425 | 236 | 3,688 |
| 68508 | Newspaper Advertising | 3-Commu | 0 | - | 1,243 | 12 | 567 | 34 | 346 | 865 | 3,467 |
| 06342 | Communication Total | 3-Commu | 4 | 12,662 | 19,330 | 12,416 | 16,505 | 13,904 | 15,136 | 28,812 | 56,965 |
| 89063 | Travel | 4-Other | 0 | 19,300 | 15,333 | 15,000 | 15,890 | 12,009 | 1,367 | 247 | 478 |
| 07421 | Phone | 4-Other | 0 | 200 | 150 | 155 | 200 | 120 | 145 | 207 | 109 |
| 93012 | Computer/Office Equipment | 4-Other | 2 | 400 | 500 | 100 | 200 | 500 | 100 | 500 | 770 |
| 24601 | Postage | 4-Other | 0 | 683 | 153 | 356 | 235 | 746 | 462 | 678 | 346 |
| 35151 | Other Total | 4-Other | 2 | 20,583 | 16,136 | 15,611 | 16,525 | 13,375 | 2,074 | 1,632 | 1,703 |
| 10460 | Benefits | 1-Personnal | 0 | 12,034 | 13,565 | 10,674 | 13,095 | 16,392 | 12,357 | 20,775 | 24,766 |
| 35246 | Payroll taxes | 1-Personnal | 0 | 345 | 347 | 154 | 1,953 | 374 | 534 | - | - |
| 76745 | Salaries | 1-Personnal | 1 | 521 | 434 | 178 | 519 | 1,850 | 543 | 764 | 133 |
| 76023 | Commissions and bonuses | 1-Personnal | 0 | 0 | 2,300 | 189 | 90 | 23 | 456 | 246 | 346 |
| 23674 | Personnel Total | 1-Personnal | 1 | 12,900 | 16,646 | 11,195 | 15,657 | 18,639 | 13,890 | 25,326 | 25,599 |
| 14678 | Web Research | 2-Marketing | 2 | 6,000 | 2,300 | 5,000 | 1,500 | 1,200 | 1,266 | 1,500 | 4,600 |
| 10567 | Independent Reaearch | 2-Marketing | 1 | 2,000 | 5,420 | 3,000 | 2,100 | 900 | 580 | 4,252 | 3,674 |

# How They Are Organized

Many databases are set up as a table. Tables have rows and columns. Each row might stand for a person. Each column could be a person's name and age.

## FAST FACT

**Big databases can have thousands of tables to store data.**

**You can store any information on a database!**

## How Data Is Found

People look for things in a database by using a **query**. A query can be words or numbers. You can search a database for every person with the first name Rick.

# Activity
# Fun with Databases

**MATERIALS**
notebook
pencil

Want to learn more about databases? Here are ways to get started:

Gather your data. Write down the names,

age, and hair color of your friends and family. You can also add other types of data. You could list favorite food and favorite color.

Make a database. Take all of your data and put it into a table. Start with the first row. Write down one person's name. Then write down their age, hair color, and so on. Make a new row for another person. Fill out the row just like you did for the first person. Continue creating rows for all the data you gathered. Now you have a database!

# LEARN MORE

## Books

Danna, Cindy. *Field Day! Represent and Interpret Data*. New York, NY: PowerKids Press, 2014.

La Bella, Laura. *How Do I Use a Database?* New York, NY: Rosen, 2014.

Towne, Isobel, and Jason Porterfield. *Strategic Searches Using Digital Tools*. New York, NY: Rosen Publishing, 2016.

## Websites

**KidsClick! Web Search**
*www.kidsclick.org*
Practice searching databases with these family-friendly web searches.

**Math Is Fun**
*www.mathsisfun.com/data/data.html*
Learn about math-related data in a fun and easy way online with examples and quiz questions.

# INDEX

Published in 2019 by Enslow Publishing, LLC.
101 W. 23rd Street, Suite 240, New York, NY 10011

Copyright © 2019 by Enslow Publishing, LLC.

**Library of Congress Cataloging-in-Publication Data**

Names: Mapua, Jeff, author.
Title: Data and databases / Jeff Mapua.
Description: New York : Enslow, 2019. | Series: Let's learn about computer science | Audience: Grades K-4. | Includes bibliographical references and index.
Identifiers: LCCN 2018002551| ISBN 9781978501812 (library bound) | ISBN 9781978502253 (paperback) | ISBN 9781978502260 (6 pack)
Subjects: LCSH: Databases—Juvenile literature.
Classification: LCC QA76.9.D32 M37 2019 | DDC 005.74—dc23

LC record available at https://lccn.loc.gov/2018002551

Printed in the United States of America

**To Our Readers:** We have done our best to make sure all website addresses in this book were active and appropriate when we went to press. However, the author and the publisher have no control over and assume no liability for the material available on those websites or on any websites they may link to. Any comments or suggestions can be sent by e-mail to customerservice@enslow.com.

**Photos Credits:** Cover, p. 1 Gorodenkoff/Shutterstock.com; pp. 2, 3, 4. 24 Best-Backgrounds/Shutterstock.com; p. 4 ESB Professional/Shutterstock.com; p. 6 Everett Collection/Shutterstock.com; p. 8 fizkes/Shutterstock.com; p. 10 razorbeam/Shutterstock.com; p. 12 Pressmaster/Shutterstock.com; p. 14 © iStockphoto.com/simonkr; pp. 16, 18 Rawpixel.com/Shutterstock.com; p. 20 wavebreakmedia/Shutterstock.com; p. 22 Syda Productions/Shutterstock.com; interior design elements (laptop) ArthurStock/Shutterstock.com, (flat screen computer) Aleksandrs Bondars/Shutterstock.com.